Five-a-side Soccer — R.W. ELLIOT

ISBN 0 7158 0543 6 (limp) ISBN 0 7158 0711 0 (hard)

CONTENTS

Page

FIVE-A-SIDE SOCCER
FOREWORD

By SIR DENIS FOLLOWS, C.B.E.
Secretary of The Football Association from 1962 to 1973.

As Secretary of The Football Association I welcomed the opportunity given to me by the National Association of Youth Clubs to write a foreword for this booklet which they have prepared to provide information for organisers and officials of five-a-side football competitions, especially those concerned with youth clubs.

During the past fifteen years there has been a steady and most encouraging increase in the number of competitions and matches played in what are termed small-side football matches. Apart from the pleasure which such games give, particularly to young players, they are recognised by the F.A. Coaching Authorities as an integral part of all worthwhile coaching schemes and it is true to say that at both National and County level five-a-side football matches are included in Coaching Course programmes. I should like to take the opportunity of assuring all those concerned that The Football Association welcomes and supports the promotion of youth activities, especially those whose interests are directed mainly towards Association Football, and the efforts which have been made to provide facilities for young people to play five-a-side football both indoors and out of doors, and to say that if any problems arise they should write to The Football Association for advice and guidance. Both the Coaching Staff and Administrative Staff at the F.A. Headquarters will be only too pleased to help in any way possible.

I send my good wishes to all members of the National Association of Youth Clubs and wish them every success in their endeavours to provide facilities so that football may be played on the widest possible scale in every town and village throughout the country.

DENIS FOLLOWS

INTRODUCTION

'...On receiving the ball from his goalkeeper he moved with it along the wall towards the opposite goal. When challenged he played the ball firmly 'wallwards' and swerved 'inside' to take the expected rebound. The light ball, however, struck a protruding collar on the battery of cast iron central heating pipes which encompassed the playing area, rebounded obliquely backwards and bounced crazily past an astonished goalkeeper into the attacking player's own net!!!'

'...A large area of plaster from the wall above the goal, weakened and shattered by countless 'near misses', collapsed without warning, completely engulfing the hapless goalkeeper below in a mound of debris, and shrouding the players, spectators and the trophies on proud display alike in a dense, choking blanket of white dust!!!'

The incidents recounted above occurred during the final event of a local Association of Youth Club's five-a-side football tournament in the north of England. The year was 1956 and the venue a redundant church hall which, though totally unsuited for indoor football, was one of the few premises available in which such an activity could be practised at that time.

Despite similar limitations elsewhere, this version of 'small-side' football flourished, particularly as an activity for boys in youth groups. It was from these humble beginnings that a major national youth five-a-side football tournament developed. This event, organised by the National Association of Youth Clubs in conjunction with its constituent local and divisional associations, has now been running for twelve years and attracts entries from some two thousand club teams from all parts of the United Kingdom.

In 1971, as part of that Association's Diamond Jubilee Year celebrations, the five-a-side football finals were staged in the magnificent main sports hall attached to the Commonwealth Games Stadium at Meadowbank, Edinburgh. The facilities provided there must equal if not excel any others existing currently in Britain. A far cry indeed from that church hall in the north of England!

Since the 1950s, organised competitive five-a-side football tournaments have proliferated, and today at a considered guess, there must be some fifty thousand teams playing regularly in such events throughout Britain. Indeed, the game must rank as the most popular 'participant' small-side team game of this century. With nationwide television coverage now being given to major championship competitions, which involve teams of well known professional players from leading league sides, the game is rapidly becoming a spectator sport too.

Six national youth tournaments are now in existence, and a growing interest in the game is being shown by girls, for whom competitive events are being organised in many areas. It is evident, therefore, that five-a-side football is here to stay as a highly competitive sport, and because of this there is a recognised need, accepted by the majority of those involved in administering the sport, to introduce some uniformity to the rules of play. These, though adhering for the most part to the basic rules laid down by the Football Association for 'small-side' games, vary considerably in some details from organisation to organisation.

If a uniform set of rules were adopted universally, then it would enable:-

1. Referees to interpret and administer the rules more consistently.
2. Playing areas and appurtenances to become more standardised, thus facilitating the production of more and better equipment and assisting those responsible for planning new sports provision to cater more adequately for the game.

Perhaps, however, the most important reason for advocating the general acceptance of standard regulations is to ensure that, as a more highly organised competitive event, the game continues to be conducted within the rules and regulations of Association Football; that is, as far as the differing conditions under which five-a-side football is played will allow. For this game, in common with other versions of small-side football, must endure as a useful adjunct to the major sport, as it is an ideal training activity eminently suited to assisting performers thereof to become more expert exponents of the game of football. Because, too, five-a-side football can be played indoors it is a game for all seasons and times. Thus it can provide perhaps the only opportunity available to many hundreds of individuals to experience the thrills and satisfaction derived from actually playing football.

One reason for producing this booklet, therefore, is to present a carefully considered and detailed set of rules of play, complying fully with the Rules of Association Football and the Laws of the Game; and based on the combined knowledge and experience of many persons actively engaged in some aspect of competitive five-a-side football.

Another reason for going to print on this subject is to provide a written commentary on a vitally exciting activity which, in this age of increased leisure, has tremendous potential. It is sincerely hoped that the information contained in the ensuing pages will interest, inspire and maybe instruct both players and planners alike!

R.W. ELLIOT

WINNING STYLE

Time and time again one finds the club attitude to Five-a-Side is that of "it's the poor relation to the real game" - what utter nonsense! One might just as well say that table-tennis is the poor relation to Lawn Tennis! It is about time that clubs realised that Five-a-Side has now become an established and recognised sport form - and treated it as such! How often do you see clubs equipping their teams with the right gear for the game? More often than not

teams turn out in jerseys taken from the 2nd or 3rd XI, any old shorts and "don't worry about socks or shoes, bring your own!" With the availability of quality soccer wear being what it is club secretaries should kit their Five-a-Side Teams with the same pride and thoroughness that they give to that other section of the sport - the Eleven-a-Side team!

This year sees the introduction of many new and exciting team strips - some available to amateur clubs for the first time. Umbro International, the manufacturers and designers of most of the original trends in top class soccer-wear, have introduced for club wear two new designs which are bound to be popular. Firstly, the contrast front panel as worn by Birmingham City, this is available in nylon and polyester fabric (ideal for Five-a-side) in a variety of colours including amber/black and royal/white. The other trendy introduction is the new European sash style which has been adopted by Manchester City as their 'special' alternative strip, the illustration we show is the all white jersey with the scarlet and royal blue sash. This jersey is made in nylon which ensures really attractive colouring and, what is more, easy washing. Whilst on the subject of jerseys we've included the scarlet/white collared style of Sunderland in our illustrations because we feel there could be quite a following for these colours - again they are available in nylon from the Umbro range.

Soccer shorts never make great news — unless they fail to stay up during a TV Match of the Day! — but the latest style worn by Chelsea have created quite a stir; these shorts with their wide contrast stripe in white on a royal background are now available to all clubs in the same cut and quality as used by the First Division Club and to add to the authenticity you'll find the famous 'flashing diamond' on the leg — the mark of the choice of champions.

What to wear on the feet is often a problem but again with the fantastic choice of nylon hose available in the Umbro '12 month guarantee' range you couldn't do better than visit your local stockist right away, but that still leaves the question unanswered as to 'shoes'. We feature the

Adidas Olympia — a light training shoe ideal for Five-a-Side especially as the natural gum rubber sole gives such a good grip — and long wear. This shoe is only one in a very big range of suitable shoes all with the famous three stripes and all within the reach of most club secretaries' funds.

Remember you can win in style and morale gives you a good head start.

THE GAME - as it is played

'It is not only a fine spectacle this five-a-side football. It is invaluable practice for positional sense, off-the-ball running and picking up somebody if you have lost the ball.'

(Sir Matt Busby)

Five-a-side football, as a competitive event, evolved from small-side training exercises practised by most professional league clubs. It is a fast, non-stop game which demands from those who play it mobility, speed and ball control.

There are no time-consuming 'throw-ins' or corner kicks, and the playing area is encompassed by four walls, or ideally, a solid surround on to which the ball is played in the same manner as is the puck in ice-hockey. Thus play is continuous and the walls used as extra defenders or attackers, depending on a given situation.

There is no off-side rule; charging an opponent is forbidden, as are violent tackles; for within the confines of an enclosed area bounded by non-resilient surfaces, the use of such tactics can be highly dangerous.

The ball must be kept below head-height at all times. This rule was introduced for two reasons:-

1. To permit high kicking in the confines of indoor premises could make the game a fiasco, as the ball could be lofted from end to end of a playing area with little effort. It could also be the cause of excessive damage to lights, ceilings, etc.

2. Keeping the ball low encourages players to develop controlled and accurate play, and to become adept at playing the ball 'off' the walls to best advantage.

This means, of course, that 'heading' the ball is restricted to 'diving' or low-bending efforts, and that the high lob cannot be used. On the other hand the speculative high kick and the wild, lofted clearance are prohibited, thus encouraging players to concentrate on perfecting precise passing techniques, for defensive, as well as attacking moves.

Although positional play is a feature of the game, players' positions are not defined, as attack and defence merge into one continuous motion. Therefore, the 'out-players' must be highly adaptable, able to 'close-mark' opponents, anticipate and intercept their passes, then when in possession, convert to an attacking role immediately. Even the goalkeepers are fully involved in this fluidity of action, for their returning of the ball into play after gaining possession is invariably their team's first move in another attack. (Fig. 1)

The successful five-a-side performer needs to develop skills such as turning quickly with the ball kept in full control, and changing direction suddenly and thus beating an opponent in a limited space. Speed 'off-the-mark' is also a necessary attribute, and as already emphasised, absolutely precise and accurate passing ability. In a game where 'possession' is all-important, one cannot afford to mis-direct a single pass - the direct consequence of which could be a score for the opposing side!

'Side-foot' passing is most accurate for the short distance, and this should be practised incessantly, using a 'pushing' movement, preferably with the inside of the foot.

Using the outside of the foot can be most effective in certain situations, e.g. to deceive opponents by suddenly changing the direction of a pass, but it is much more difficult to master than 'inside of the foot' play and usually less accurate. (Fig.2)

For long passing, and shooting at goal, the ball must be hit firmly with the instep. At 'impact' the body should be leaning slightly forward with the knee over the ball, thus ensuring that it keeps low. It should be remembered when practising shooting that, initially, direction is more important than velocity. (Fig.3)

Turning the body at an angle to the 'target' and kicking 'across' the surface of the ball rather than directly into it, causes it to swerve in flight. This tactic can be used to

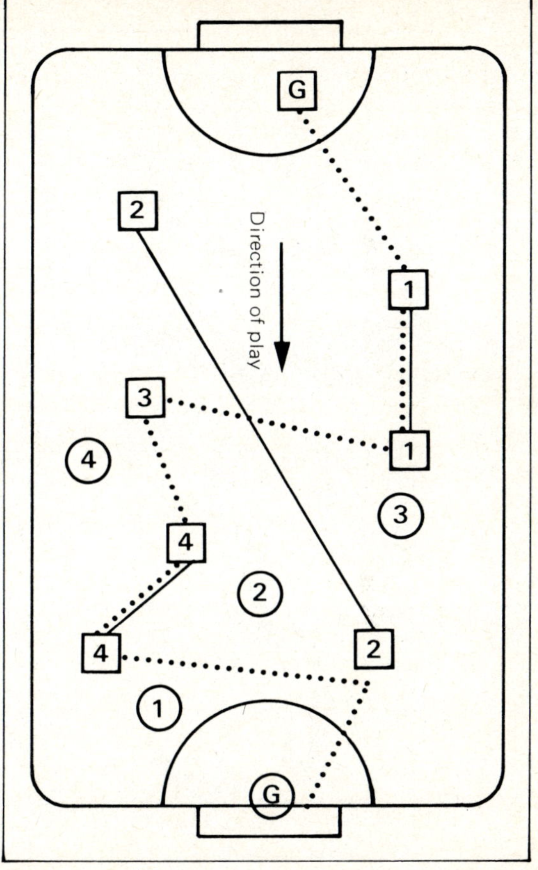

Fig.1 Build-up of an attack from clearance by goalkeeper.

(Dotted line indicates path of ball; solid line, path of player running into position without ball. Both lines together indicate player moving with ball.)

deceive goalkeepers and for 'curving' passes round an opponent.

Playing the ball off a wall or barricade is a unique feature of five-a-side football and can be deployed to great advantage in both attack and defence. (See Figs. 4 & 5).

Practising this technique, therefore, is a necessary feature of training and Fig.6 illustrates a useful exercise to help develop skills in striking the ball so that it rebounds at the desired angle and speed.

High-scoring games in five-a-side football competitions are no more prevalent than in the major game, and as might be expected, the successful long shot is a rarity - though, nonetheless, spectacular when it does find the net. Goals are usually scored as a culmination to a series of passing movements in which skilled positioning 'off the ball' is as important as the action of the player in possession. Individual efforts often achieve success too, and a break-through dribble always provides exciting play for spectators.

Training methods, therefore, should be primarily aimed at developing in players a high standard of ball control and an ability to out-manoeuvre opponents in a confined space. The 'team dribble game', illustrated in Fig.7, with its many variations, is recommended as an ideal exercise to help players acquire such qualities.

Fig.2 Passing with the side of the foot.

Fig.3 Shooting.

Players stand 1 metre (3ft.approx) apart, behind 'team' lines. At a given signal, player no.1 of each team runs to starting line for ball, then proceeds to dribble it round the remaining players (Diagram A) *or* plays it against wall or barricade (Diagram B) between each player. Returning along the line is the same in each version, i.e. dribbling round each player and returning the ball to the starting line. The game is completed when all team members have repeated the action as described, and the team to assume its original position first, with the ball on the starting line, is the winner.

OTHER VARIATIONS. Objects, e.g. chairs, can be used to dribble round, in which case the teams line up behind the starting line with the ball at the feet of player no.1, both at the commencement and finish of the game.

The ball to be played through the players' legs in one direction.

A combination of all the above versions can be used in one exercise and of course single teams can race 'against the clock'.

The best possible training exercise for goalkeepers is to be fully involved in team-shooting practice. Skill in gathering the ball should be perfected as a 'palmed' or diverted shot

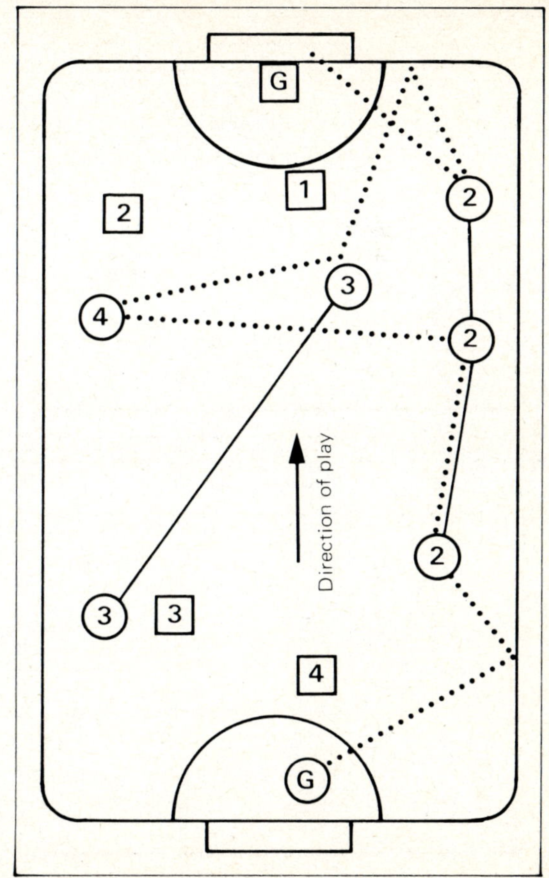

Fig.4 Using wall/barricade for attack.

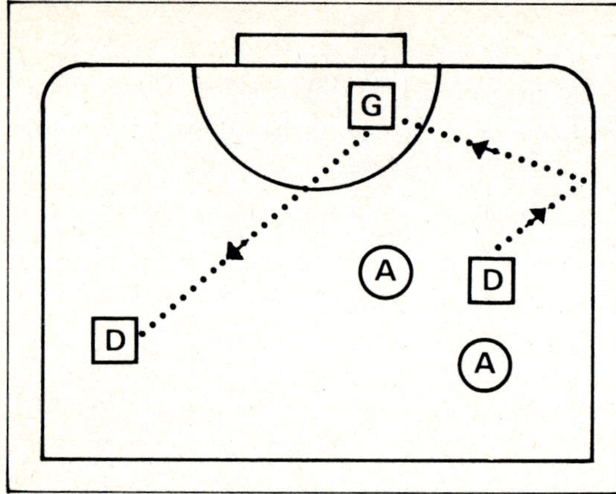

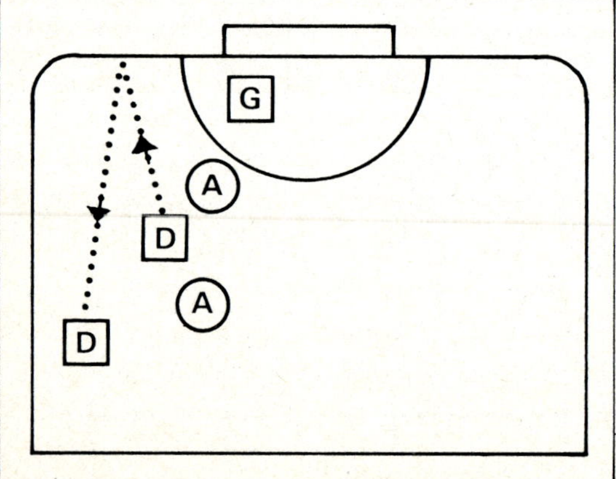

may well rebound from the surrounding walls to present another scoring chance to the opposition. The 'rebound practice' illustrated in Fig.6 could apply to goalkeepers too, who would roll instead of kick the ball against the wall. This would help to improve their skill in distribution - which iş almost as important as preventing goals from being scored.

Goalkeepers should wear knee bandages or tracksuit trousers in play, as constant falling on hard surfaces can cause severe bruising at least.

Five-a-side football is becoming exceedingly popular as a girls' activity and many competitions for girls' teams are now in existence. This is not surprising as women's participation in Association football has increased greatly in recent years. In fact the Women's Football Association has now been officially recognised by the F.A. and this could mean a proliferation of ladies teams and competitions. Because deliberate bodily contact is prohibited in the five-a-side version of the game, it is possible that girls are attracted more readily to it. Present trends seem to indicate that this small side game could become a major sport for women in the seventies. No modifications of rules or conditions of play are necessary for competitions involving women's teams. However, it is generally accepted by those with some experience of women's football that, for

Fig.5 Using the barricade for defence.

(In both situations the defender is 'caught' in possession, facing own goal).

MOVEABLE
OBJECT
(eg Chair)
PLAYER No. 1
PLAYER No. 2

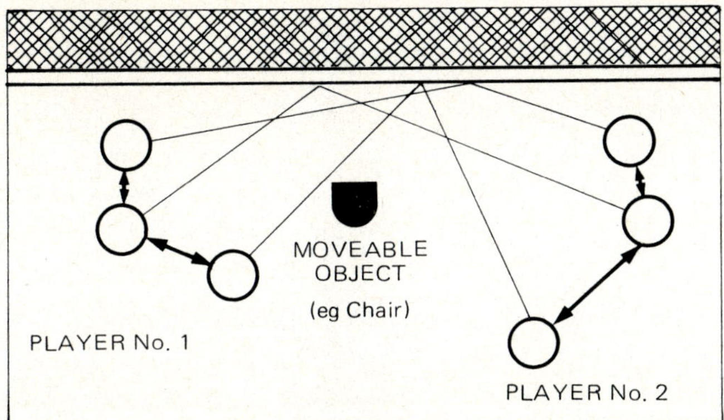

Fig.6 Rebound practice involving 2 players.
(Moveable object should be placed nearer or farther from wall as desired)

beginners anyway, there is need for special coaching in side-stepping and swerving in order to avoid head-on collisions between players. Girls do not seem to take evasive action as naturally as boys, and this may be due, in part, to the fact that their childhood games gave less opportunity to practise such movements.

The team dribble game, as described previously (page 11) is strongly recommended as a means of rectifying this short-coming, together with match experience of course. Girls

(A)
(B)
WALL OR BARRICADE
TEAM LINES
5 metres
(16ft. approx.)
STARTING LINES
BALL
BALL
KEY
Player without ball
Play with ball
Ball only

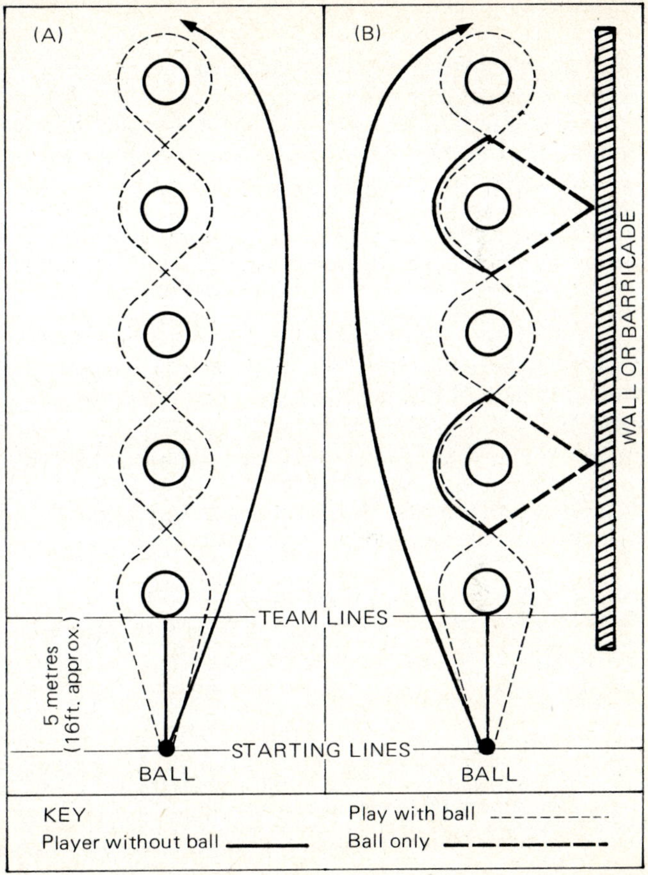

Fig.7 Version of team dribble game (with variation)

too, like young boys, often need coaching in the correct technique of applying foot to ball.

The rather controversial question as to whether girls playing football need more bodily protection than boys, cannot be ignored. There is no doubt that the impact against the body of a ball driven hard, from close quarters, can be quite considerable. In five-a-side football all players, and particularly goalkeepers, receive such blows frequently. Because, therefore, many girls fear the consequences of incessant knocks on, or about, the breasts, those playing the game should be encouraged to wear brassieres which give maximum protection. Protective 'cups' as used in fencing, supported by a normal-type 'bra' would also offer a defence against the ball or collisions with other players.

Pre-match tactics talks and exercises are just as apposite to five-a-side as to Association football. Figs. 8 to 14 illustrate basic, tactical moves, and hints on positional play which could be practised in training sessions.

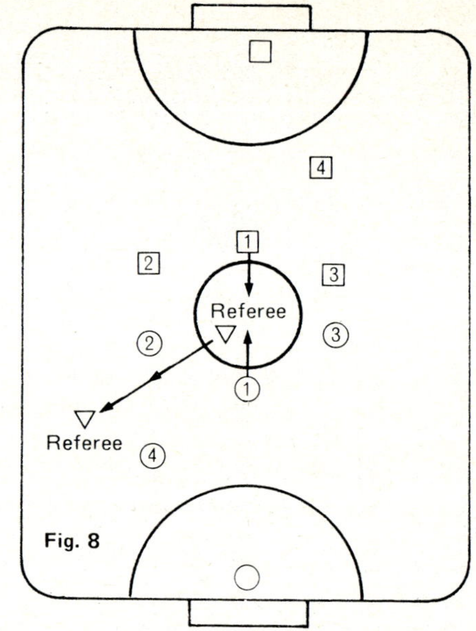

Figure 8 - The Kick-off. Suggested 'line-up'.
The No. 1 players on each side should be ready to move forward and challenge for possession as soon as the ball touches the ground after being 'dropped' by the referee. All other players should be prepared to move immediately into defence or attack, depending on which side gains possession first.
N.B. In order that he impedes play as little as possible it is suggested that the referee moves away from the centre circle immediately play commences.

Figure 9. Mounting an attack from a 'kick-off'; (or from re-start after a goal has been scored).
Attacker No. 1 reaches the ball first and plays it out to his right, where colleague No. 3 has moved up to take possession. When challenged by Defender No. 4, Attacker 3 plays the ball across the arena to his No. 2 who had moved forward as soon as his side gained possession, and is now in an unchallenged shooting position.
Notes for Defenders. Always mark those opponents who are 'off' the ball, but seeking empty spaces!

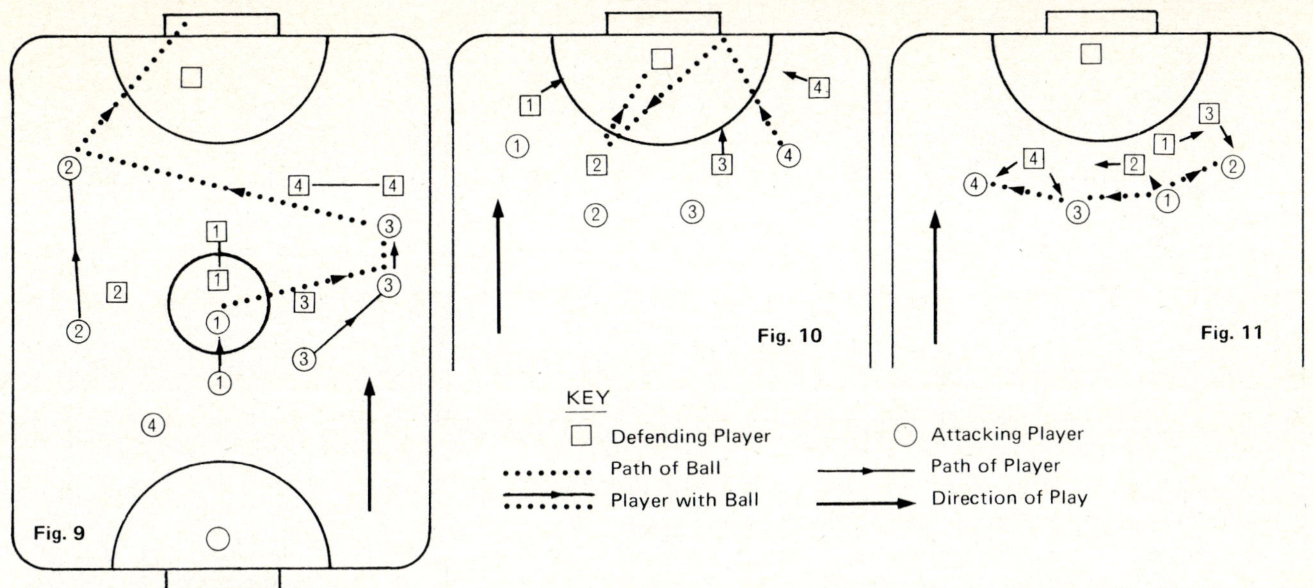

Figure 10. Defensive Positions (1)
Defenders, under attack, should stand facing own goal when opponents are shooting. This is so that resultant rebounds can be returned directly to the goalkeeper for clearance, thus avoiding the difficult and often dangerous manoeuvre of a Defender having to turn with the ball in possession in order to clear his lines! e.g. Attacker No 4 breaks through to shoot, and hits goal post; the rebound is played immediately back into the goalkeeper's hand by Defender No. 2.

Figure 11. Defensive Positions (2)
To meet free kick being taken from in front of goal, Defenders Nos.1 and 2 should form a 'wall' between Attacker No.1, who is taking the kick, and the goal. Defender No.3 should take up a position slightly to the left, and be prepared to challenge Attacker No.2, if he receives the ball from the kick. Defender No.4 should be ready to move either to the left or right to counteract Attackers No.3 or 4. The goalkeeper should take up a position towards the right of his goal, and be ready to move forward to 'narrow the angle', should one of the Attackers break through into a shooting position.

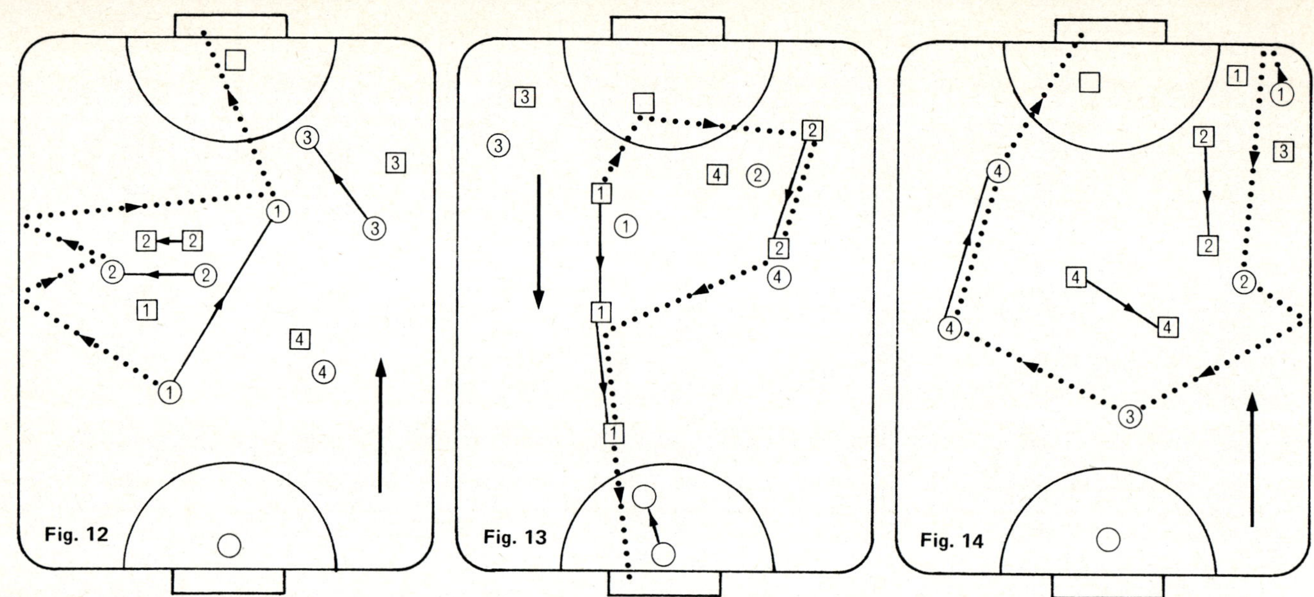

Figure 12. Attack from 'set piece' i.e. free kick
Attacker 1, seeing colleague closely marked, hits ball firmly against nearest wall, and immediately runs forward into a shooting position. Attacker 2 moves across to receive rebound and flick it first time on to wall, taking Defender 2 with him – thus leaving Attacker 1 clear to meet second rebound, and shoot at goal; (NB. Attacker 3 has moved forward to edge of goal area on right to meet possible third rebound).

Figure 13. Turning defence into attack from a set piece, i.e. free kick
Defender No.1 plays free-kick back to goalkeeper, who rolls the ball out to his only unmarked colleague, Defender 2; he moves forward with the ball and when challenged by Attacker No.4, passes into the open space on his right, where the ball is met by Defender No.1 who has moved forward into that space, thus gaining a clear run to goal.

Figure 14. Using barricades to evade close-marking defence
Attacker No.1, on being 'cornered' plays ball against end wall, so that it rebounds to colleague No.2, behind him. This player, also closely-marked, plays the ball *first-time,* against the side wall so that it rebounds to the rear where Attacker No.3 is unmarked. He immediately transfers to colleague No.4 so that he can make for goal before the defence re-groups.
Note to Defenders. If Attacker No.1 had not been so closely marked in the first place, he may have been tempted to shoot for goal, and at that angle the shot should have been easily covered by the goalkeeper.

Play in Partially Enclosed, or Completely Open Areas

As stated elsewhere, by far the greater proportion of match, five-a-side football takes place in areas not completely enclosed by walls or barricades. Quite often, in buildings like aircraft hangars, for instance, pitches have no surrounds at all, as is the case with many outdoor venues. For the most part however, in gymnasia and club halls, the usual pattern is that both 'goal-ends' are enclosed by the walls of the building, but one, or both touch lines, are defined only by floor markings. Under such conditions it is inevitable that the ball is put 'out of play' on many occasions during a game. This necessitates having 'roll-ins' to restart play, i.e. a player rolling the ball back into play with an underarm action whilst keeping both feet outside the touch line; (see page 39 - Rule 12 — 'Ball in Play' — Note 2)

In order to compensate for actual playing-time lost by the ball going out of play, games, ideally, should be of longer duration than those played within an entirely enclosed arena; the exact timing depends on the extent to which continuous play is possible in any venue, and of course it is realised that in tournament events, extensions of playing time are only possible if the total time available to play the required number of games is adequate.

The following suggestions are offered as a guide to those responsible for planning events on partially enclosed pitches:-

1. In arenas with three sides enclosed, (i.e. *one* touch line, or goal line, only 'open') — TWO EQUAL PERIODS OF *NOT LESS* THAN 8 MINUTES.

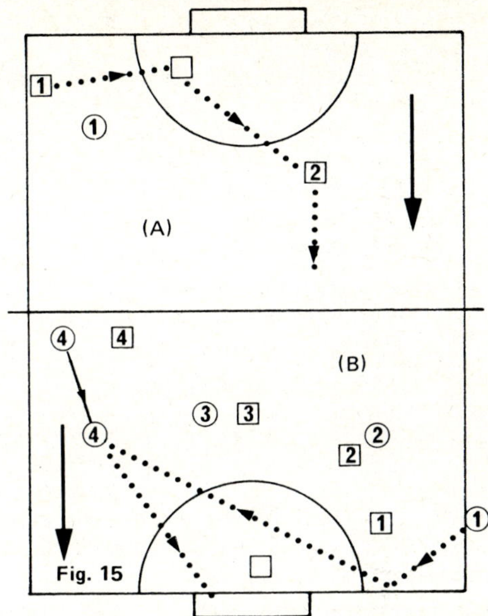

Figure 15. Using 'roll-ins' for defence and attack
(a) Defender 1, closely marked in corner, 'rolls' ball to goalkeeper, who in turn transfers ball to unmarked colleague.
(b) **In area with end wall enclosed**
Attacker 1, rolls ball hard against end wall to evade 'marking' defenders. Attacker 4 moves quickly forward to meet rebound.

2. In arenas with:-
   (a) TWO 'GOAL-ENDS' enclosed (i.e. both touch lines 'open'), or
   (b) *ONE* 'goal-end' and *ONE* touch-line enclosed. (i.e. the other goal-end and touch-line 'open'); or
   (c) *TWO* touch-lines enclosed. (i.e. two goal-ends 'open') – TWO EQUAL PERIODS OF *NOT* LESS THAN – 10 MINUTES.

3. In arenas which have no enclosed sides – (i.e. both touch lines and goal-ends 'open').
   TWO EQUAL PERIODS OF NOT LESS THAN – 15 MINUTES

Apart from the above modifications, games on partially enclosed and totally 'open' arenas can be conducted exactly as recommended in the subsequent sections of this book. Referees should insist that 'roll-ins' are promptly and correctly taken, and as with throw-ins in the game proper, these can be used to great advantage in both defensive and attacking situations (see Fig.15).

Touch lines and goal lines should be clearly marked (see Rule 1 – 'The Playing Area') and when spectators are present organisers should ensure that such markings remain clearly visible at all times. The practice of placing over-turned forms, or gym-benches along the touch or goal lines should be discouraged, however, as these can constitute a great danger to players.

Notes

1. A goal cannot be scored direct from a roll-in, and if the ball so propelled does cross the goal line between the posts without being played by another player, then, if it was an attacker who took that roll-in, play is resumed by the goalkeeper rolling the ball out. If a goal results directly from a roll-in by a defender then a 'corner' roll-in is awarded to the opposing side; i.e. the ball is rolled-in from the point where the goal line and touch line meet on the side nearest to where the ball entered the goal in the first place.

2. Because of the limitations of the 'roll-in', viz. the ball must be propelled with an underarm action and kept below head-height, and the confines of the areas in which five-a-side football is played, the progress of play can be seriously impeded if opponents insist on standing too close to a player taking a roll-in. Referees should treat such actions as obstruction and deal with them accordingly.

THE GAME - as it is staged and controlled

'Football indoors is a fast, skilful and exciting game - and in one evening it is possible to stage a knock-out competition with 12 to 16 teams taking part -'

(H.R.H. The Duke of Edinburgh)

The following chapters were compiled only after extensive research had been undertaken, involving:-

a. Preparing a questionnaire on organisation, equipment and administration. This was completed by twenty-five youth worker colleagues involved in five-a-side football tournaments in their different areas of operation throughout Britain.

b. Examining and comparing the rules of play applying to six national youth tournaments and obtaining the comments and opinions of the organisers thereof.

c. Consulting with other experts, e.g. referees, and staff members of sports halls with considerable experience of competitive events.

d. Observing a great number of actual games being played under a variety of differing conditions and rules of play, and consulting with players and spectators thereby encountered.

e. Obtaining the comments and opinions of experts from firms involved in the design and/or manufacture of sports equipment.

NOTES

1. The Football Association rulings preceding the ensuing sections of this chapter relate to 'Laws for Small Side Matches or Competitions', as printed in the current F.A. Handbook, and are reproduced by kind permission of the Football Association.

2. All measurements are given in metric terms with approximate equivalents in feet and inches.

THE PLAYING AREA

'Five-a-side football may be played in an enclosed area, either indoors or outdoors'

Since 1965 some fifty to sixty multi-purpose sports complexes have been put into commission in England and Wales, and a further two hundred will be available for public use within the next ten years. Similar progress in this field can be expected with regard to Scotland.

These developments, together with the improved facilities for indoor physical recreation being attached to educational establishments generally are providing the playing areas on which the game of five-a-side football continues to flourish.

Despite such advances, however, there still exists a great dearth of premises suitable for playing the game, to anything like competition standard. This situation will persist in many areas for some time to come and so rules and playing regulations for competitions must remain as flexible as possible to allow for local variations.

At the same time, because of the widespread interest in the game, and because many local events serve as qualifying stages for regional and national tournaments it is most desirable that an attempt be made to effect some standardisation of the conditions under which five-a-side football is played. If such uniformity could be achieved 'the planners' may be encouraged to consider purpose-built playing areas as an integral feature of future sports complexes.

Also, as the game has all the attributes of an excellent spectator-sport, it is sincerely hoped that in future planning some thought will be given to providing suitable accommodation for spectators.

Floor surfaces are usually of wood and maple-sprung floors are ideal. However, granwood, composition-vinyl, or the more recently introduced P.V.C. covered flooring, have been found to be equally practicable. Solid-based surfaces, like concrete or tarmac without any covering, can be dangerous and gravel-topped areas when dry are exceedingly dusty and unpleasant. Pitches which are part of a large floor-area, as in airfield hangars, for instance, are proved to be affected by condensation in humid weather conditions. This causes surfaces to be extremely slippery for players wearing rubber-soled shoes. Playing areas need to be well illuminated and fluorescent lighting is suitable for most halls. Those units which fix directly into the ceiling, and with re-inforced glass covers, are most appropriate, and where spot-lights are used, these need to be so positioned that neither players nor spectators are affected by 'glare'.

Pitch markings should be durable and easily distinguishable from both the natural floor colouring and the markings for other games. Because there is no off-side rule in five-a-side football, and because a goal can be scored from any part of the pitch, apart from the goal areas, it is not necessary to mark a half-way line. A centre 'spot' is needed however on which the ball is 'dropped' to commence a game. A circle of 1 metre (3 ft. approx.) radius marked round the centre spot, would assist the start-of-play rules to be observed.

In order to comply with the special rule concerning the taking of penalty kicks, which allows for the goalkeeper's heels only to be on the goal line, it is suggested that the front edge of the line between the goal posts should protrude not more than 5 cm (2'' approx.) on to the playing area. This will enable the goalkeeper to stand upright, if so desired, unimpeded by the low crossbar.

2. SURROUNDING WALLS OR BARRICADES

Though small-side football team games can, and indeed do, take place on open areas, both indoors and out, the five-a-side version is played to best advantage on an enclosed pitch where the surrounding walls or barricades make continuous play possible. These walls should be firm; of smooth surface; without breaks or protruberances, and in the interests of safety, not less than 1.06 metres (3 ft.6in. approx.) in height.

Ideally, goals should be so constructed that the posts are in line with the barricade and not protuding on to the playing area. Where such positioning is not possible, curved corner-pieces as illustrated in Fig. 16 are recommended. Such accessories help preserve the continuous character of the game, by preventing the ball from becoming lodged in the side netting of the goal. Similarly, if the corners of playing areas were rounded, the fluidity of play would be further enhanced. It is strongly recommended that future purpose-built provision should be designed with rounded corners, and that adaptations to produce the same effect in existing pitches be made wherever practicable.

In the majority of multi-purpose sports-halls and gymnasiums the actual structural walls form the surrounds for a five-a-side football pitch. Often the presence of doorways and wall-fittings of one sort or another are impediments to continuous play. Unless there are conveniently placed recesses in the end walls, the goals must protrude onto the playing area. If space permits, the erection of temporary surrounds ought to be considered, especially if competitive events are being staged. Trestle-table tops, if securely fixed and using the trestles as supports, can make a serviceable barricade. At the Meadowbank Sports Centre in Edinburgh,

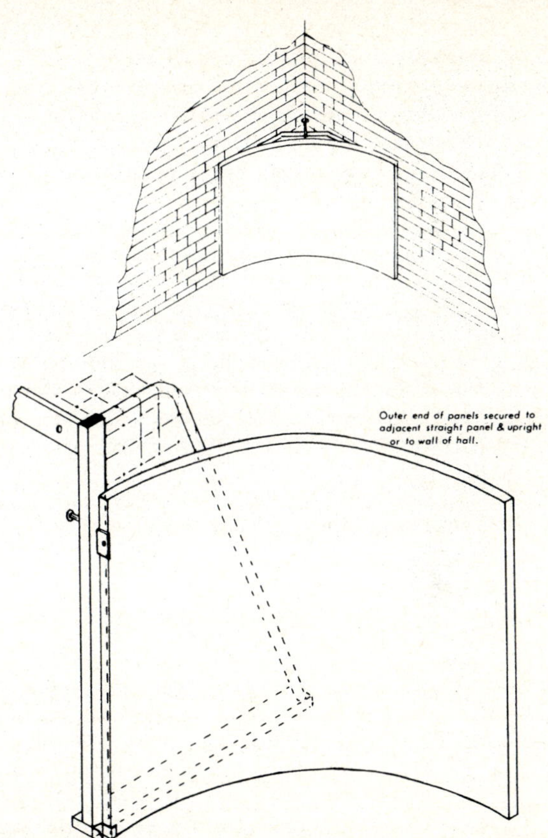

Fig. 16 Corner units and their application.

portable wooden counter-type sections are used to form most adequate surrounds. These are 2.5 metres (8ft) long and 500 mm (2ft) wide and there are some smaller sections to fill any gaps. The back of the sections are open and shelved, thus providing useful storage facilities. They can also be used for catering purposes. (See Fig.17)

Most highly recommended are portable surrounds comprising lightweight, cellular-core, hardboard (or white melamine) faced panels, 2.7 metres (9 ft.) in length and 1.06 metres (3 ft. 6 in.) high. These sections are supported and linked by light, square-tube, metal posts and crossbars, and secured by floor clamps of special design. Together with the curved, corner pieces, described previously (Fig. 16), and according to particular needs, either complete or part surrounds, can be constructed from these units.

The diagram on page 29 (Fig. 21) illustrates the ideal playing area.

3. THE GOALS

'The goals are 16 feet long by 4 feet high'

The height of five-a-side goals, as stipulated by the F.A. ruling above, is generally accepted for competition purposes. The distance between the goal posts depends on the size of the playing area and varies considerably, from a minimum 2.4 metres (8 ft.) for a local tournament in Lincolnshire, to a maximum 5.5 metres (18.ft.) at the Empire Pool, Wembley where the National and London championships are staged. The pitch dimensions there, however, are exceptional, being 62 metres (200 ft.) by 26 metres (85 ft.).

For most other major tournaments, which are staged on playing areas of 50 feet and upwards in width, the stipulated goal-width is 5 metres (16 ft.approx.). It would appear, though, again from evidence received, that for junior events involving players aged 13 years and under, a reduction of width to 3.5 metres (12 ft.) is favoured.

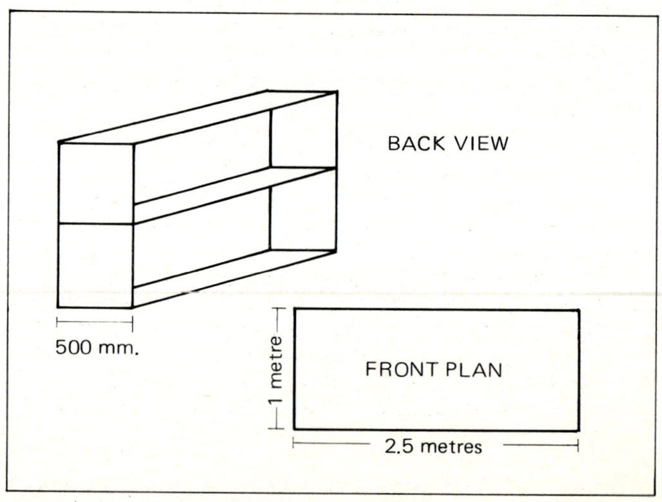

Fig. 17 Counter-type surrounds

Construction can be of wood or tubular metal, and in most cases, the 'units' need to be portable, and if possible, collapsible for storage purposes.

Nets are most essential in order to ascertain when a goal has been scored, for in the majority of playing areas the goals are backed by a hard surface from which the ball rebounds at great speed. Goal nets should be of sufficient depth to enable the ball to travel *at least* 60 cm (2 ft.) beyond the goal line, and should have sufficient clearance to the rear so that the ball does not strike a wall and rebound on to the playing area.

The goal unit illustrated in Fig. 18 fulfils all the above requirements and is considered most appropriate for a multi-purpose playing area. It is light, portable and sectional for easy storage, and the tubular steel-end frames will support a 2.5 metres (8 ft.), or 3.5 metres (12 ft.), or the regulation 5 metres (16 ft.)-long aluminium crossbar, according to particular needs.

4. THE BALL

'The ball used is Size 4'

In the ultimate rounds of the majority of major national tournaments a size 4 football is used, but for the most part in other competition events, the type of ball played with is dictated by the limitations of the premises in which the games are staged.

A leather ball can do a great deal of damage to plastered walls, windows, lights and other furnishings common to club rooms, church halls and school gymnasiums. Therefore

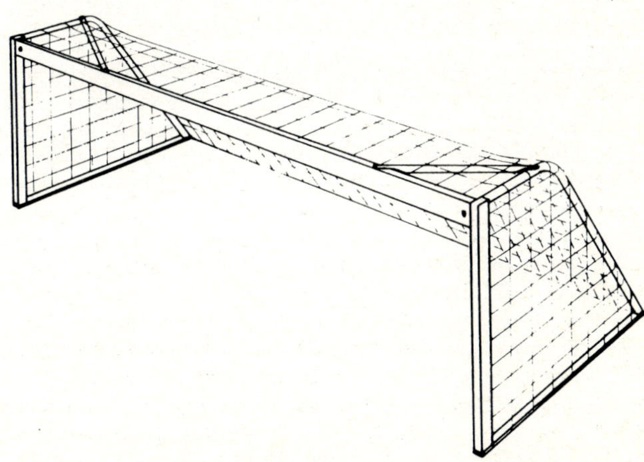

Fig. 18 Goal Unit

the lightweight (8½ oz. - 0.25 kg approx.) plastic ball, which is cheap in price and more expendable than the leather ball, is still used extensively in local five-a-side competitive events, and in the preliminary stages of larger tournaments.

In the light of experience, which is supported by the evidence obtained, it is recommended that,for the final stages of major competitions, at least, a size 4 leather football or its equivalent be used. This ball (which weighs between 12 and 13 ozs.) is considered to be the most appropriate for the game IF NOT FULLY INFLATED. Recommended pressure is 0.5 kg per square cm (7lbs per square inch, approx.).

Experiments have been conducted to test different types of balls under tournament conditions. These resulted in the players and officials involved agreeing unanimously that a specially manufactured size 4 leather ball, by Mitre Sports, inflated to a pressure of 0.5 kg per square (7 lbs. per square inch) was ideal for the game. The other balls used were an ordinary leather-panelled football, size 4, and both a rubber and a plastic equivalent thereof. Each ball was played with on at least 5 different occasions, and for each period of play they were inflated to different pressures. At the end of the experiment none of the balls used showed appreciable damage or wear. Other evidence considered suggests that with prolonged use a leather ball wears more quickly than either a rubber or a plastic ball. The colour of the ball too is quite important, as in confined, indoor conditions backgrounds vary considerably. Unless, therefore, the ball is distinctively coloured, players and officials do often experience great difficulty in following its flight. Though, in the writer's experience white is probably the most distinguishable colour, against light coloured surrounds and floors, a white ball too can become 'lost' in the background. Red and orange clashes too frequently with players' strips and floor surfaces so it could well be that an entirely black ball would prove most distinguishable for indoor playing areas.

(NOTE: To test for the pressure required without a gauge, place the ball on the ground and press firmly with both hands, fingers and thumbs expanded. Without exerting undue force the thumbs should make depressions of approximately 1 cm (½ inch) in depth in the surface of the ball).

5. PLAYERS' EQUIPMENT

Except for footwear, the dress for five-a-side football is the same as that worn in the major game. Girls, however, may prefer a distinctive design of strip combining comfort and ease of movement, with a fashionable style. Fig. 19 illustrates such apparel, designed by Mr. G. Erik of Subbuteo Sports Games Ltd., and is presented as a prototype for girls' five-a-side dress.

Because of the non-resilient surfaces with which players can come into forcible contact, the danger of wearing anything that could cause injury is stressed. Buckles, bracelets and rings all come into this category.

With regard to footwear, there is, as borne out by the evidence to hand, a considerable divergence of opinion as to what should or should not be allowed in five-a-side football. Changing circumstances under which the game is being played and the introduction of the light-weight training shoe to the sporting scene, have given rise to the modification of the rules of some competitions, which hitherto, had stated quite unequivocably that *'-only plimsolls; i.e. rubber soled shoes with canvas uppers,* would be allowed-'. In situations where playing areas are of minimum size, surrounded with 'damageable' furnishings, and where a light-weight ball must be used, then such a rigid rule is obviously still necessary. However, the introduction of the heavier ball in larger arenas demands that players should be a little more 'heavily shod', and many types of modern training shoes, whilst offering more substantial protection to the feet, constitute little extra threat to other players than did, for instance, the previously widely accepted baseball boots.

It is recommended that included in tournament regulations are notes giving guidance as to the type of footwear permissible. The referee should be the final arbiter, however,

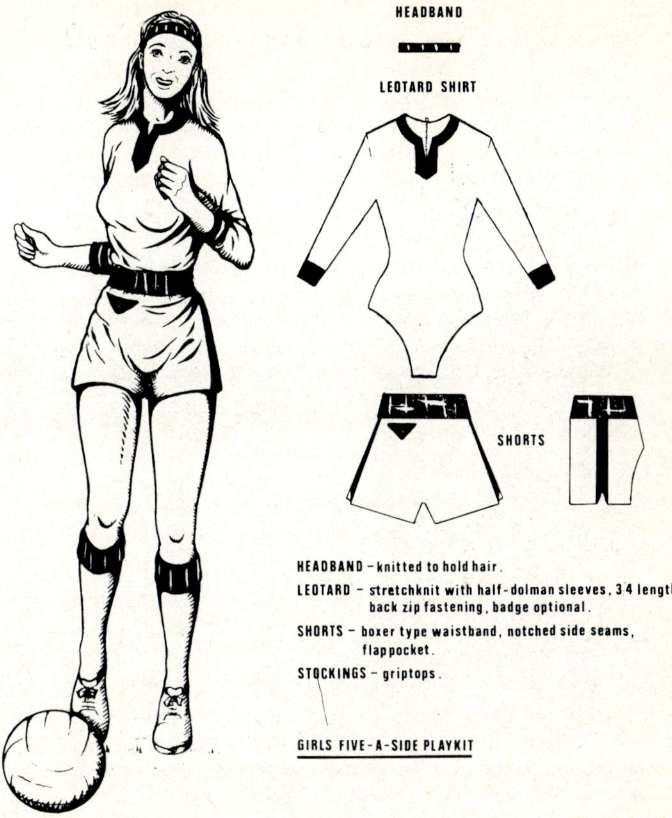

Fig. 19 Girls' playing strip.

(Designed by G.Erik)

as to whether or not shoes worn by any player constitute a danger to others. Experience gained from many years of involvement in tournament play suggests that though a great deal of pre-match emotion is often displayed over the type of footwear worn by members of opposing teams, seldom do players deliberately seek unfair advantage by wearing shoes that could cause injury to others.

A tracksuit is a very useful accessory to a player's equipment. Not only is it needed for the inevitable delays which occur between games in tournament events, but the trousers thereof can be worn in actual play to protect the limbs against bruises and cuts. Players, in particular goalkeepers, who are susceptible to such injuries should also wear an elastic knee bandage or pad.

6. DURATION OF PLAY

F.A. Rule – *'- Six minutes each way: in the event of extra time being required, play will continue until the first goal -'*

There seems to be general agreement amongst tournament organisers that the above timing is about right for competitive five-a-side events. Playing in this fast non-stop game indoors and often under hot musty conditions can be most tiring.

'- Although these games are fairly short, they can be more hectic and tiring than some 90 minute matches on full-sized pitches - I remember leaving the arena last year; I was exhausted, and my feet were killing me! -'

So commented a world-famous international player after his first experience of five-a-side tournament soccer.

It is considered that three or four 12 minute matches are about the maximum a player can manage in one period of three hours or so. One must also allow for the extra time which may be needed to settle drawn games.

7. DRAWN GAMES

For settling drawn games, two methods are in general use. In knock-out events, the 'penalty system' is favoured, i.e. alternate penalties are taken by players of each side in turn, and immediately one side has registered more goals with the same number of kicks taken, then that side is declared the winner - e.g. with the score standing at 2 penalty-goals to each side, player no.3 of Side 'A' shoots and misses; player no.3 of Side 'B' then takes his penalty and scores. Side 'B' has therefore won the game, and no more penalty shots are taken.

The other method is for the two teams involved to commence another full game, which is terminated as soon as a goal is scored. The side scoring that goal is declared the tournament winner. If this 'extra' game is also drawn, then either the penalty system as described previously is put into operation, or the tournament declared a 'tie'. Both methods are equally acceptable, but because invariably time is at a premium in five-a-side tournaments, the penalty system of settling a drawn game is more frequently adopted.

8. REFEREEING

As with the eleven-a-side game, one referee officiates in five-a-side and he is the sole arbiter in matters concerning the rules of the game. To control such a fast, fluid activity, complete concentration is needed. Unless decisions are made and action decided spontaneously, then the play can be adversely affected, as situations develop so quickly. In order to assist the referee to maintain this concentration, an independent time-keeper/scorer - sometimes two persons - officiates in tournament play.

The game is commenced when the referee drops the ball, as per rules, but at half-time and full-time the signal for ending play is given by the time-keeper. Generally a whistle is used, but in order to distinguish the time-keeper's signals from those given by the referee, a bell or buzzer is sounded. In some well-equipped halls an electric buzzer-type signal is automatically sounded when time runs out. A large time-clock, as used in ice hockey, and illuminated score-boards, both visible to players and spectators alike, help to enhance the game. If the referee has to stop play other than at half-time or full-time, e.g. for injury or disciplinary reasons, then if deemed necessary, he will use a pre-arranged signal to indicate to the time-keeper that time be suspended until play resumes again.

In five-a-side football, a referee is not primarily concerned about 'keeping up with the play', but in keeping out of the way of it! He will need to move quickly and often in order not to obstruct the players, but at the same time adopt positions where he can turn quickly and see all the play with a minimum of movement. Extravagant gesticulations and needless running can distract both players and spectators alike.

Play is usually least concentrated in the centre of the field and it is suggested that the referee operates mainly from there (See Fig. 20). He should on no account position himself close to the surrounds or too near the goal area, for it is in such positions that he could impede play considerably.

The referee should check the goal and nets very carefully before play commences, for often one of his most difficult tasks is to decide, in case of doubt, whether or not a goal has been scored. For example, if the back of the net is close to a wall or barricade, then a hard-hit ball can rebound into play, possibly before the referee can move from a position he has taken up some distance away. The same problem can arise from the goalkeeper fumbling a quick shot and the question is whether he allowed the whole of the ball to cross the goal-line before it was recovered. Only keenness of eye, judgement and concentration will enable the referee to make the correct decision, but noting previously the exact nature and position of the nets and back walls in relation to the goal posts, will help.

He must be very strict from the outset in dealing with heavy tackling and charging, for within the confines of a playing area bounded by non-resilient surfaces, such play can be highly dangerous. If he has any doubt about the safety of articles of dress or equipment, he must take action to have these removed immediately. Shoes with hard, non-resilient uppers or barred or studded soles should be prohibited, and dangerous protruberances on walls, barricades or goals either removed or insulated.

Refereeing five-a-side football is just as onerous and demanding as participating in the game proper. Absolute concentration is necessary whilst a game is in progress, and in tournament events, a single referee ought not to be expected to take game after game without relief. Where more than three matches are to be played successively, then two officials ought to be appointed, and for 10 games and upwards, three referees are needed.

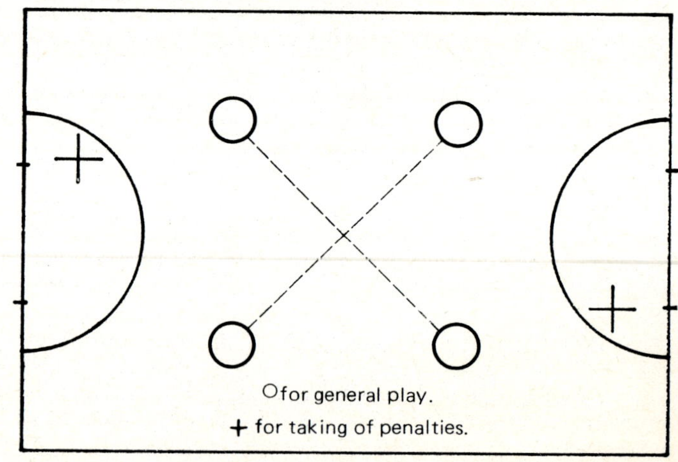

Fig. 20 Suggested refereeing positions.

RECOMMENDED RULES FOR INDOOR FIVE-A-SIDE FOOTBALL COMPETITION EVENTS

In accordance with the Laws of the Game of Association Football and based on 'Laws for Small-side Matches or Competitions', as stated in 'Rules of the Association and Laws of the Game' (F.A. Handbook).

NOTE Where it is thought necessary, the full text from the Laws of the Game of Association Football appertaining to the relevant sections is reproduced in some detail.

RULE 1 - THE PLAYING AREA

The Playing Area, and the markings thereof, shall be as shown in Fig.21.

DIMENSIONS

LENGTH	Maximum 36 metres (120 ft.)
	Minimum 30 metres (100 ft.)
WIDTH	Maximum 28 metres (90 ft.)
	Minimum 18.5 metres (60 ft.)

MARKINGS

All markings should be durable (i.e. painted or 'taped'), distinctive (i.e. in contrast to the natural floor covering) and lines should be not less than 5 cm (2 ins.) and not more than 7.5 cm (4 ins.) in width.

a. CENTRE MARKING – A suitable mark to be made in the exact centre of the playing area on which the ball is 'dropped' to commence a game. The Centre Spot shall be surrounded by a circle 1 metre (3 ft.) in radius.

b. GOAL AREA – A semi-circle of 7.5 metres (25.ft.) radius shall be drawn from the centre of each 'end' of the playing area. The extremities of these semi-circles

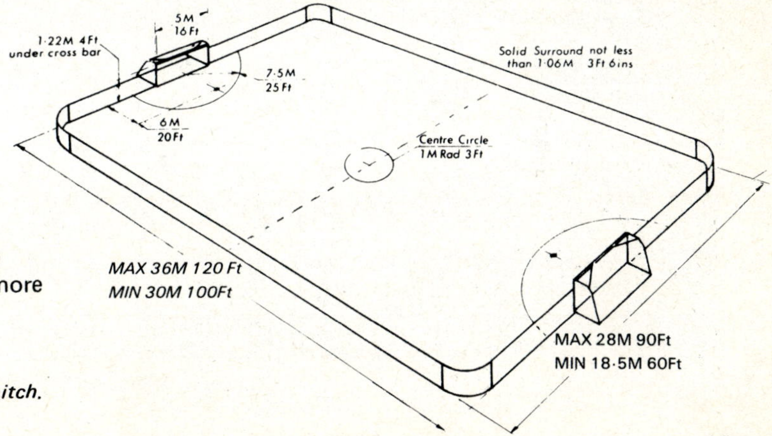

Fig. 21 Dimensions of whole of pitch.

A N.A.Y.C. Five-a-side Final in progress.

should reach the wall or barricade REGARDLESS OF WHETHER OR NOT THE GOAL POSTS ENCROACH ON TO THE FIELD OF PLAY *(see Fig.21).*

c. GOAL LINE – The front edge of the line drawn between the goal posts shall protrude NOT MORE than 5cm (2 ins.) onto the playing area. (See Rule 8 - Penalty Kicks)

d. PENALTY SPOT – Penalty 'spots' should be made at 6 metres (20 ft.) from the centre of each goal line.

THE GOALS

These shall be placed in the centre at each end of the playing area and should consist of two upright goal posts joined by a horizontal crossbar 5 metres (16.4 ft.) long, the underside edge of which is 1.2 metres (4 ft.) from the surface of the playing area. The goal line i.e. the line drawn between the goal posts should coincide with the goal post in width, except that the front edge of the line should protrude not more than 5 cm (2in.) on to the playing area (see Rule 8 - Penalty Kicks). Nets should be attached to the goals and these should extend to not less than 60 cm (2 ft.) behind the goal line.

N.B. Wherever possible, goal posts should be in line with the barricade or recessed into the end wall and not encroach on to the playing area.

VARIATIONS IN PITCH DIMENSIONS

The following scaling down of dimensions is suggested for playing areas which do not conform to the above rule:-

For areas of *less than 30 metres (100 ft.) long and 18.5 metres (60 ft.) wide,* the GOAL AREA should be reduced to a semi-circle of *6 metres (20 ft.)* radius, and the WIDTH OF THE GOALS reduced to *3.5 metres (12 ft.).* The PENALTY SPOT should remain at *6 metres (20 ft.)* from the centre of the goal line and the mark made on the radius of the semi-circle.

For areas of *less than 24 metres (80 ft.) long and 15 metres (50 ft.) wide,* the dimensions should be for GOAL AREA a semi-circle of *5.5 metres (18.ft.),* for GOALS *3.5 metres (12.ft.)* in width, and PENALTY SPOT *6 metres (20 ft.)* from the centre of the goal line and OUTSIDE the goal area.

For juniors (i.e. under 14 years of age) it is suggested that, on a pitch of maximum dimensions, the width of the goals is reduced to *3.5 metres (12 ft.),* all other dimensions remaining as stated in the rule. On smaller sized playing areas no amendment to dimensions of the goal is considered necessary.

RULE 2 - THE BALL

The construction of the ball shall comply with the requirements stipulated in the Laws of Association Football, i.e. *'The ball shall be spherical; the outer casing shall be of leather or other approved materials. No material shall be used in its construction which might prove dangerous to the players'.*

The size of the ball shall be equivalent to a Size 4 football (i.e. weighing between 339 grammes and 367 grammes (12 to 13 ozs.) and of circumference between 60 cm and 62 cm (25 to 26 in.).

The ball should NOT be fully inflated, i.e. not more than 0.56 kg per sq.cm (8 lbs. per sq.in.), and not less than 0.50 kg per sq.cm (7 lbs. per sq.in.).

It is strongly recommended that for all classes of competitive play the ball used be as stipulated.

RULE 3 - NUMBER OF PLAYERS

a. A game shall be contested between two teams, each having not more than 5 players, one of whom is a goalkeeper.

b. ONE substitution per team to be permitted at any time during a game, subject to the same conditions as in Association Football (see NOTES).

c. The goalkeeper may change places with another player (or the named substitute) during a game providing the referee is notified of this change BEFORE it takes place.

d. The decision as to the minimum number of players which should constitute a team is left to the governing body of a competition, but it is recommended that a match should not be considered valid if there are fewer than THREE players in either team involved.

NOTES

1. The referee shall be informed of the name of the substitute (if any) before the start of the match.

2. A substitute may only enter the playing area during a stoppage in the game and when the referee has given a signal authorising such entry. The game should not be re-started if the player being substituted is still in the playing area AND THAT PLAYER SHALL NOT TAKE ANY FURTHER PART IN THE GAME.

3. If a player is ordered from the playing area by the referee (a) BEFORE A GAME IS STARTED The named substitute may take that player's place BUT the start must NOT be delayed to allow the substitute to join the team. (b) AFTER A GAME HAS BEEN STARTED That player may NOT be replaced.

   If the named substitute is ordered off either BEFORE or AFTER play has commenced, NO replacement of that player is permitted.

   N.B. The above does not apply to players ordered off to remove or correct articles of apparel. They may rejoin the game when such instructions have been complied with to the satisfaction of the referee.

4. A substitute is deemed 'a player' and as such is subject to the referee's jurisdiction whether that player has actually played in the game or not.

RULE 4 - PLAYERS' EQUIPMENT

a. A player may not wear anything which constitutes a danger to other players.

b. Colours worn by the goalkeeper MUST be distinct from the colours worn by any other players.

c. FOOTWEAR. Lightweight footwear shall be worn, without rigid or hard soles, bars or studs.

NOTE. If the referee judges footwear or any other article of apparel to be a danger to other players participating then the player concerned shall be ordered to replace or remove same. If this instruction is not carried out to the referee's satisfaction then that player shall not take part, or take no further part, in the game.

RULE 5 - REFEREES

A referee shall be appointed to officiate in each game, who shall have the same powers and duties as those laid down in the Laws of Association Football.

NOTES (from F.A.Laws of the Game).

The referee shall:-

1. Enforce the rules and decide any disputed point. His decision on points of fact connected with the play shall be final so far as the result of the game is concerned. His jurisdiction begins from the time the game commences and his power of penalising shall extend to offences committed when play has been temporarily suspended. He shall, however, refrain from penalising in cases where he is satisfied that by doing so he would be giving an advantage to the offending team.
2. Have discretionary power to stop the game for any infringement of the rules and to suspend or terminate the game whenever, by interference by spectators, or other cause, he deems such stoppage necessary. In such a case he shall submit a detailed report to the competent authority, within the stipulated time, and in accordance with the provisions set up by the National Association under whose jurisdiction the match was played. Reports will be deemed to be made when received in the ordinary course of post.
3. Have discretionary power, from the time he enters the playing area, to caution any player guilty of misconduct or ungentlemanly behaviour and, if he persists, to suspend him from further participation in the game. In such cases the Referee shall send the name of the offender to the competent authority, within the stipulated time, and in accordance with the provisions set up by the National Association under whose jurisdiction the match was played. Reports will be deemed to be made when received in the ordinary course of post.
4. Allow no person other than the players to enter the playing area without his permission.
5. Stop the game if, in his opinion, a player has been seriously injured; have the player removed as soon as possible from the playing area, and immediately resume the game. If a player is slightly injured, the game shall not be stopped until the ball has ceased to be in play.
6. Have discretionary power to suspend from further participation in the game, without previous caution, a player guilty of violent conduct.
7. Decide that the ball provided for a match meets with the requirements of Rule 2.

RULE 6 - TIMEKEEPERS/SCORERS

An independent time-keeper/scorer shall be appointed to assist the referee. This official shall:-

a. Record goals scored
b. Act as time-keeper, and signify half-time and full-time by an agreed signal.
c. Suspend time, at the referee's instructions, for all stoppages, and add that time to the end of each half.

RULE 7 - DURATION OF THE GAME

The duration of a game shall be two equal periods of SIX MINUTES, subject to the following:-

a. Allowances shall be made in either period for time lost through stoppages, as decided by the referee, and recorded by the time-keeper.

b. Time shall be extended to permit of a penalty kick being taken at, or after, the expiration of the normal period in either half. The half-time period shall not normally exceed two minutes.

EXTRA TIME. In competitions being staged on a 'knock-out' basis, games ending in a draw at the expiration of full-time are decided by playing two extra periods of TWO MINUTES EACH. If the scores are still level after extra time EITHER:

(i) A further game is commenced which continues until a goal is scored. The team scoring that goal being declared the winners, OR

(ii) PENALTY KICKS. (see Rule 14) Players of each side in turn (except the goalkeeper) shall take penalty kicks alternately until one side leads the other in goals scored with an equal number of kicks taken. If after the four 'out-players' in each side have taken TWO penalty kicks each (a total of EIGHT kicks per side) the score still remains level, then a further series of kicks should be taken from 7.5 metres (25 ft.), i.e. from the centre of the line marking the goal area circumference. The kicks shall be taken at each goal with the four 'outfield' players of one side shooting, as described, at the goal-keeper from the other. Whilst awaiting their turn to shoot, the players shall remain outside the goal areas.

(If another referee is not available, then the official in charge of the game being decided MAY authorise the time-keeper to supervise the penalty kicks being taken at one goal.)

c. COMMENCEMENT OF ANOTHER GAME which will terminate immediately a goal has been scored, and the team scoring that goal declared the winner.

   If the game is still level at the end of this further game, then yet another game of THREE MINUTES EACH WAY should be commenced OR the game decided by penalty kicks as described in (a) above.

NOTE: THE METHOD TO BE ADOPTED TO DECIDE DRAWN GAMES MUST BE DECIDED BY THE ORGANISERS AND NOTIFIED TO THE REFEREE PRIOR TO ANY GAMES IN A TOURNAMENT BEING COMMENCED.

RULE 8 - THE START OF PLAY

a. At the beginning of a game the choice of 'ends' will be agreed by mutual consent of the teams involved OR by the toss of a coin, if so desired by either of the said teams.

b. Play will begin by the referee 'dropping' the ball in the centre of the playing area between ONE player from each side, each of whom will stand not less than 1 metre (3 ft.) from the centre marking. The ball will be deemed in play and the game commenced when the ball has touched the ground. No player should move towards the ball until it is 'in play'. If the rule is not complied with then the referee shall repeat the procedure.

c. After a goal has been scored, and after half-time, when the teams will change ends, the game will be re-started in like manner.

d. After any other stoppage the game will be re-started by the referee 'dropping' the ball, as described above, at a point nearest to where the ball was when play was suspended - UNLESS it was in the goalkeeper's possession, when that player will, at the referee's signal, 'roll' the ball out to re-start the game. The referee will not 'drop' the ball nearer than a point 2 metres (6 ft.) from the lines marking the goal areas, or from surrounding walls or barricades.

NOTE. In accordance with the Laws of Association Football, if a player infringes any of the rules before the ball is 'in play', the player shall be cautioned or dismissed from the playing area, depending on the nature of the offence committed. A free kick cannot be awarded to the opposing team, however, as the ball was not in play at the time of the offence. In such circumstances the referee will again 'drop' the ball to start the game.

RULE 9 - BALL IN AND OUT OF PLAY

The ball shall be in play at all times from the start of the game UNLESS -

a. THE BALL RISES ABOVE HEAD-HEIGHT (this height to be at the referee's discretion). N.B. The heading of the ball is allowed, providing the aforementioned condition is observed.

b. A goal has been scored, i.e. the ball wholly crosses the goal line, between the goal posts and under the crossbar, either on the ground or in the air.

c. The time-keeper has given the signal for half-time or full-time.

d. The game is stopped by the referee for an infringement, injury to players, or for any other reason.

PENALTY FOR INFRINGEMENT. An INDIRECT FREE KICK against the offending team from the point where the ball was last played UNLESS -

i The ball was last played by the defending goalkeeper in the goal area, in which case the INDIRECT FREE KICK shall be taken from a point not less than 2 metres (6 ft.) OUTSIDE the goal area, nearest to where the offence occurred.

ii The ball rebounds to above head-height from any of the following situations:-

From a player who has made no attempt to play the ball.

When the ball is adjudged by the referee to have been played simultaneously by opposing players.

From a wall, barricade, goalpost, crossbar or other obstructions.

THEN the referee will re-start play by 'dropping' the ball between two opposing players at the point where the rebound occurred. If this point is in the goal area then the re-start takes place, as described above, NOT LESS THAN 2 metres (6 ft.) outside the goal area nearest to where the rebound occurred.

iii The ball goes over the barricade surrounding the playing area without rising above head-height.

NOTES

1. If the ball goes over a barricade surrounding the playing area (except for those parts of it enclosed within the goal areas) without rising above head-height, then play shall be re-started by the referee 'dropping' the ball at a point within the playing area nearest to where it went out of play, but NOT LESS THAN 2 metres (6 ft.) away from the barrier.

When the ball crosses the barricade behind the goals and within the parts of the barricade enclosed in the goal areas, again without rising above head-height, then play is re-started by the goalkeeper defending the goal in question 'rolling' the ball out (see Rule 12).

2. When it proves necessary to play on areas without surrounds, and the ball goes out of play, i.e. the whole of the ball crosses one of the lines marking the extremities of the pitch, then play should be resumed by a player from the opposite side from that to which the player who last touched the ball belongs, rolling the ball with an underarm action, and with both feet outside the playing area, back into play from the point where the ball crossed the line.

If a defender plays the ball over his own goal-line, i.e. between the goalposts and the corners of the pitch, then a player from the attacking side rolls the ball back into play, as described above, from the corner nearest to where the ball crossed the goal line. If an attacker plays the ball over the opponents' goal line, then play is re-started by the goal-keeper 'rolling' the ball out.

(As the absence of surrounds makes the game much slower, duration of matches should be increased to at least 15 minutes in each half; or to at least 8 minutes in each half if the playing area is partially enclosed. See page 18.)

RULE 10 - SCORING OF GOALS

A goal is scored when the WHOLE of the ball crosses the goal line between the goal posts and beneath the crossbar UNLESS-

i It was thrown, carried or intentionally propelled by hand or arm by a player of the ATTACKING side, OTHER THAN THE GOALKEEPER from within that side's goal area.

ii It was last played by a player of the ATTACKING side whilst within either goal area.

The team scoring the greater number of goals, shall be the winner. If the game is goal-less, or each side scores an equal number of goals, then the game is termed a 'draw'.

RULE 11 - OFFSIDE

There is NO offside rule. Players can position themselves in any part of the playing area, except the goal areas, in which only the defending goalkeeper can be.

RULE 12 - FOUL PLAY AND MISCONDUCT

NOTE. PLAYERS CAN ONLY BE PENALISED IF ANY OF THEIR ACTIONS WHICH APPEAR TO CONSTITUTE FOUL PLAY, AS DESCRIBED BELOW, ARE, IN THE OPINION OF THE REFEREE, COMMITTED INTENTIONALLY.

a. FOUL PLAY means, a player:-

- i Charging an opponent. (NO CHARGING OF ANY KIND IS ALLOWED)
- ii Kicking or attempting to kick an opponent.
- iii Tripping, i.e. throwing or attempting to throw an opponent by the use of the legs, or stooping in front of, or behind, him.
- iv Jumping at an opponent.
- v Striking or attempting to strike an opponent.
- vi Holding or pushing an opponent by hand or any part of the arm.
- vii Handling the ball, i.e. carrying, striking or propelling the ball by hand or arm. (THIS DOES NOT APPLY TO THE DEFENDING GOALKEEPER WITHIN THE GOAL AREA)

For each of the above offences A DIRECT FREE KICK is awarded to the opposing team from the point where the offence occurred.

b. MISCONDUCT means, a player:-

- i Entering or leaving the playing area at any time during a game (except through accident) without first obtaining the referee's consent.
- ii Persistently infringing the rules of the game.
- iii Showing, by word or action, dissent from any decision given by the referee.
- iv Is guilty of ungentlemanly conduct (e.g. deliberate time-wasting, shouting at an opponent or spectator, etc.).

For the above offences the referee shall administer a caution to the offender.

c. FOR THE FOLLOWING OFFENCES:-

- i Playing in a manner considered by the referee to be dangerous.
- ii Intentionally obstructing an opponent when not playing the ball.
  THIS INCLUDES STANDING WITH PART OF THE BODY AGAINST A SURROUNDING WALL OR BARRICADE IN ORDER TO
  - a. PREVENT AN OPPONENT FROM REACHING THE BALL, OR
  - b. OBTAIN POSSESSION OF THE BALL FROM AN OPPONENT.
- iii Indulging in tactics which, in the opinion of the referee, are designed merely to hold up the game in order to give an unfair advantage to the team to which the player concerned belongs.

—an INDIRECT FREE KICK will be given against the offending player, to be taken by the opposing side from the place where the infringement occurred; UNLESS it is the goalkeeper who so offends whilst within his own goal area. In this case the kick shall be taken from a point 2 metres (6 ft. approx.) outside the goal and nearest to where the offence occurred.

d. A player shall be DISMISSED FROM THE PLAYING AREA if that player:-

- i Is, in the opinion of the referee, guilty of violent conduct or serious foul play.

ii Uses foul or abusive language.
iii Persists in misconduct after having received a caution.

NOTES

1. When play is stopped in order to administer a caution, OR to dismiss a player from the playing area, play shall be resumed by an INDIRECT FREE KICK awarded to the opposing side, to be taken from the point where the infringement occurred - UNLESS the player being cautioned, or sent off, or any other player, has been guilty of foul play as described in section (a) above. In this case, a DIRECT FREE KICK shall be awarded to the opposing side.

2. A player dismissed from the playing area shall not be allowed to take any further part in the game in which the offence occurred, and if there are ensuing games being played in connection with the same tournament/competition ON THE SAME DATE as the game in question, then the ban shall extend to all such games.

3. No substitution is allowed for a player dismissed from the playing area for misconduct during the game in which the offence occurred, but a substitute may be played in any ensuing games.

Whether or not the offending player is allowed to take part in subsequent rounds/sections of the same tournament/ competition in which the offence occurred or in other such events usually depends on the rules of the particular tournament/competition, and the nature of any disciplinary action taken by the governing body concerned.

RULE 13 - FREE KICKS

As in Association Football, both DIRECT and INDIRECT free kicks can be awarded for infringements of the rules (i.e. DIRECT, from which a goal can be scored without the ball being played by other than the kicker; INDIRECT from which a goal cannot be scored unless another player touches the ball before it enters the goal).

NOTES

1. When either a direct or indirect free kick is being taken no player of the OFFENDING SIDE shall stand within 2 metres (6 ft.) of the ball.
2. All free kicks (except penalty kicks) given against the defending side for infringements committed in or near the goal area shall be taken from a distance of not less than 2 metres (6 ft.) OUTSIDE THE GOAL AREA at the nearest point to where the offence was committed.

RULE 14 - PENALTY KICKS

These shall be taken from the penalty mark and, except for the defending goalkeeper, only the player taking the kick can enter the goal area, and for that purpose only.

Whether or NOT a goal is scored from the kick, the player concerned must leave the goal area immediately, and before taking any further part in the play.

The defending goalkeeper must stand , without moving his feet, and with part of both feet touching the goal line, until the ball is kicked. If necessary, the time of play shall be extended at either half-time or full-time to allow a penalty kick to be taken.

NOTE: By extending the front edge of the line between the goal posts into the playing area (see Rule 1 (c)) the goalkeeper can then stand upright if he so desires, in front of the low crossbar, by having his heels only touching that line.

RULE 15 - GOALKEEPER RETURNING THE BALL INTO PLAY

After gathering the ball the goalkeeper must IMMEDIATELY return the ball into play with AN UNDERARM BOWLING ACTION, and keeping it below head-height.
PENALTY FOR INFRINGEMENT An INDIRECT FREE KICK to the opponents from a distance of 2 metres (6 ft.) outside the goal area at the nearest point to where the offence was committed.

RULE 16 - PLAY WITHIN THE GOAL AREA

ONLY the defending goalkeeper is allowed within the goal area, EXCEPT when a penalty kick has been awarded, and then ONLY THAT PLAYER of the attacking side nominated to take the kick can enter the goal area (see Rule 8).

The defending goalkeeper must remain within the goal area at all times.

PENALTY FOR INFRINGEMENT

- i By players of the DEFENDING side, other than the goalkeeper:
  A PENALTY KICK to the attacking side.
- ii By players of the ATTACKING side:
  A DIRECT FREE KICK to the defending side from a point 2 metres (6 ft.) outside the goal area and nearest to the point of entry.
- iii By the defending goalkeeper:
  A DIRECT FREE KICK to the attacking side from a point 2 metres (6 ft.) outside the goal area and nearest to the point of egress.

NOTE

1. Referees will distinguish between accidental and intentional entry into or egress from, the goal area. Only deliberate actions, where the player either plays the ball or attempts to play the ball, will be penalised. Accidental entry or egress by the goalkeepers will be ignored providing that the player, unless injured, leaves or returns to the goal area immediately.

2. The rules of the competitions examined during the course of the enquiry undertaken, indicated a divergence of opinion obtaining over the rule affecting the goalkeepers' movements.

After further consultations, involving organisers, referees and players, the concensus of opinion was in favour of the rule confining the goalkeepers to their respective areas. Too often, it was considered, goalkeepers tended to exploit the privilege of leaving their goal areas, into which other players were prohibited from entering, to employ 'last-resort' defensive tactics, e.g. to attempt wild clearances, or challenge attacking players in the congested corner areas. Such actions were adjudged to be wholly obstructive and not in keeping with the objects of the game.

ORGANISATION OF TOURNAMENTS AND LEAGUES

Five-a-side Football competitive events take two major forms. One is the knock-out competition where teams are paired off in the first round and the winners are again paired off in each subsequent round until ultimately two meet in the final. The other is the league or American tournament system whereby each team involved in a competition plays against each other team entered and winners are decided on a points system. Because single games take only minutes to play-off, whole rounds and sometimes entire tournaments are completed on one occasion. National competitions with large entries are usually organised in stages, with successful teams progressing from, say, local to county and then to regional ties. Each regional winner thereby qualifies to participate in a final play-off event, from which the national champions emerge. In such tournaments, depending on the number of entries in each area and the local facilities available, a combination of the two systems described above is often used. Because, however, a team can be dismissed finally from a major event organised on a knock-out basis, by losing in the first round and thus only playing ten or twelve minutes football in all, league-type systems of deciding events are preferred whenever circumstances permit.

AMERICAN TOURNAMENTS

These are league-type competitions played-off usually over a single period, e.g. an evening, a whole day or a weekend. Each team plays every other team involved once, and fixture lists, similar to those used for normal league competitions, are prepared. The following sample tables illustrate how such fixtures are drawn up.

KEY–

1. Read down vertical columns for sets of games.
2. AB means Team A versus Team B.
3. The team indicated under the word 'bye' will not play in that particular set of games.

				Total Games
3 Teams				
AB	CA	BC		
bye	bye	bye	Each team	
C	B	A	plays 2 games	3
4 Teams				
AB	CA	AD	Each team	
CD	DB	BC	plays 3 games	6

5 Teams

BA	AC	DA	AE	CB	
CD	BE	EC	BD	ED	
bye	bye	bye	bye	bye	Each team
E	D	B	C	A	plays 4 games 10

6 Teams

BA	AC	DA	AE	CB	
CD	BE	EC	BD	ED	Each team
EF	DF	FB	CF	AF	plays 5 games 15

7 Teams

AB	CA	AD	EA	AF	GA	BG	
CD	DB	BC	FB	BE	EC	CF	
EF	GF	EG	GC	DG	FD	DE	
bye	bye	bye	bye	bye	bye	bye	Each team
G	E	F	D	C	B	A	plays 6 games 21

8 Teams

AB	CA	AD	EA	AF	GA	AH	
CD	DB	BC	FB	BE	EC	BG	
EF	GF	EG	GC	DG	FD	CF	Each team
GH	HE	FH	HD	CH	HB	DE	plays 7 games 28

NOTES

1. When it proves impossible to avoid a team playing in successive games, then a time lapse of at least 10 minutes between these games must be allowed.
2. The tables can also be used to prepare 'home and away' fixtures by reversing order of teams, e.g. BA instead of AB, and repeating.

TIMING. When playing games of six minutes per half duration, ONE minute must be allowed for an interval between halves and TWO minutes between games.
Thus each completed game will take 15 MINUTES and in estimating the length of a tournament the number of games to be played must be multiplied by 15 minutes, and 30 minutes added to the total arrived at for exigencies, e.g. extended intervals for teams playing in successive games, injuries, etc.

Thus the number of teams entered in an event and the time available decides whether or not a league-type competition is possible. By dividing entries into two leagues, however, the winning team in each meeting in a final play-off to decide the championship, the time taken to complete a whole tournament can be halved. For instance, if there is an entry of 7 teams then 21 games must be played if each team is to meet every other team once. Therefore, using the formula described above the tournament will last 5¾ hours. By forming two leagues of 4 and 3 teams there will be 6 and 3 games to play respectively, plus a final tie, making a total of 10 games. Using this method, therefore, the entire tournament could be completed in 3 hours.

Using more than one playing area simultaneously will, of course, further decrease the time taken to complete a series of games being played under the league system. However, it must be remembered that the time saved is not directly proportional to the number of pitches used, as the incidence of teams playing successive games becomes more frequent, thus necessitating longer intervals being allowed for between games.

League records are kept as follows:-

	P (games played)	W (games won)	L (games lost)	D (games drawn)	F (goals for)	A (goals against)	P (pts.)t
Team A	4	2	1	1	9	6	5
Team B	4	2	2	0	7	5	4
Team C	4	1	2	1	6	9	3

In the event of two or more teams gaining an equal number of points, the team having the highest goal average shall be placed higher in the league table than the other teams concerned, e.g.

Team A Goals for, 36. Goals against, 18. Goal average 2.
Team B Goals for, 54. Goals against, 22. Goal average 2.45.
Team C Goals for, 25. Goals against, 36. Goal average .69.

The order in which the above teams would appear in a league table would be: Team B - first; Team A - second; Team C - third. Where goal averages are exactly equal then a play-off must be arranged, or the competition adjudged to be a tie. Any queries, claims or protests should also be made at once in writing to the league secretary.

KNOCK-OUT COMPETITIONS

The initial number of teams entering, if not an exact power of 2, viz. 8, 16, 32 and so on, must be made so by.means of byes. The number of byes to be given is calculated by subtracting the number of entrants from the next highest multiple of 2, e.g.

3 entrants (4-3) - 1 bye - 1 game - Round 1
5 entrants (8-5) - 3 byes - 1 game - Round 1
7 entrants (8-7) - 1 bye - 3 games - Round 1
9 entrants (16-9) - 7 byes - 1 game - Round 1
11 entrants (16-11) - 5 byes - 3 games - Round 1
23 entrants (32-23) - 9 byes - 7 games - Round 1

Pairing-off is achieved by a draw, which involves placing slips with names of entrants in a suitable receptacle and withdrawing each in turn, the first one out being paired with the second, the third with the fourth, and so on.

Where byes are involved it is customary, but not essential, that the pairs who must play-off in the first round of the tournament are drawn first. Then all those remaining, after the requisite number has been drawn, become byes and go 'into the hat' together with the winners of the play-offs, to be drawn again for the second round. In most large-team, knock-out events, when each tie is played at different venues, over a period of time, the first team of a pair to be drawn out usually has the privilege of staging the tie on home ground. For most small-side and individual tournaments taking place at one venue and often during one short period of time, the whole draw from Round 1 to the Final Tie is undertaken before the tournament commences.

For example, an event involving 9 entrants would be arranged as follows:- 9 slips bearing names of entrants would be placed in 'the hat' and the first two to be drawn would play-off in Round 1 (16-9 = 7 byes). The entrant named on the next slip would play against the winner of that first round tie in Round 2 and the 6 other entrants paired to complete Round 2. Ensuing rounds need not be drawn, as will be seen from the following example of a games chart compiled from the draw:-

Where large numbers of entrants are involved, work can be minimised by numbering each entrant and using numbered slips or discs, which are easily made or purchased, for the draw.

The draw should be made if possible by a neutral person and, wherever possible, in the presence of some of the entrants or their representatives.

KNOCK–OUT COMPETITIONS

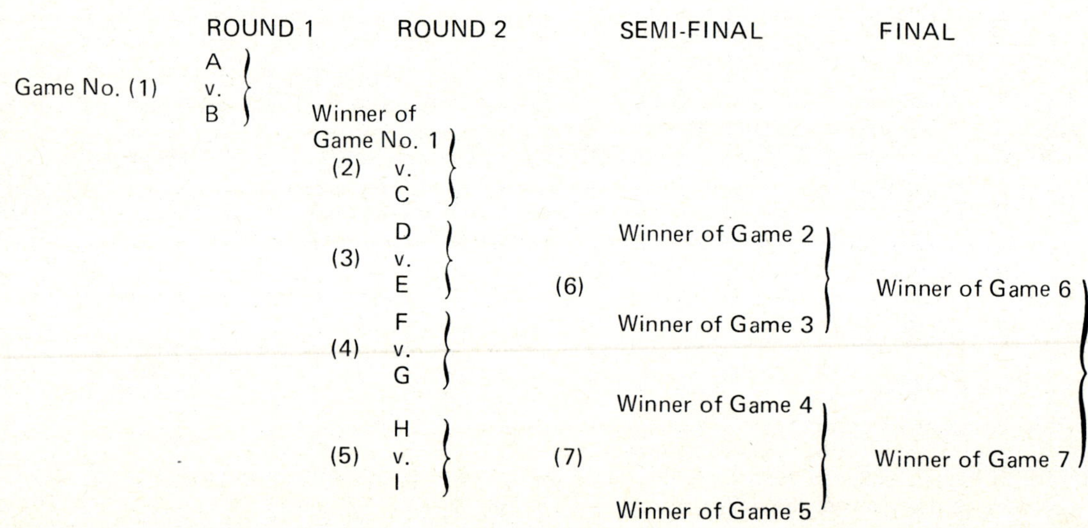

If, as in the Wimbledon Lawn Tennis Championships, 'seeding' of teams is required, i.e. ensuring that outstanding entrants do not meet until final rounds (if they survive), then in making the draw as described above the names of such teams must be withheld and written at intervals on game charts, with other entrants being drawn in order and placed on the chart, as in following example:-

Chart for 11 entrants including 3 'seeded' teams (- 16 - 11 = 5 byes):

	ROUND 1		ROUND 2	SEMI-FINAL	FINAL
	Seed No.1				
	v.				
(1st draw)	B		Seed No.1		
			v.	Seed No.1	
(2nd draw)	C		D		
	v.				
(3rd draw)	D				
					Seed No.1
(4th draw)	E				
	v.				
	Seed No.3		Seed No.3		
			v.	Seed No.3	
		(5th draw)	F		
		(6th draw)	G		
			v.	G	
		(7th draw)	H		
				v.	
		(8th draw)	I		
			v.		
			Seed No.2	Seed No.2	Seed No.2

Proper result slips and scoring charts should be made out and all results initialled by referee or umpire.

It is important that the rule stating the method to be adopted to settle drawn games be known to all teams and officials (especially the referees) prior to a tournament commencing. In timing the event too, the possibility of more than one game ending in a draw at the end of normal time ought to be anticipated.

GENERAL ADMINISTRATION

Organisers of major Five-a-side Football competitions need to be competent administrators, as a great deal of routine and often rather thankless work is involved. Rules of play and conditions of entry need to be clearly and concisely expressed and circulated to all concerned well in advance of a closing date for entries. Then the various stages of the competition have to be decided before the process of organising actual events is begun. This includes often the setting up of area groups and/or the finding of individuals who will be responsible for progressing the local, preliminary stages of the competition. Suitable venues need to be found and often adaptations must be made to rules because of the limitations of the varied types of premises which have to be used.

OFFICIALS

Match officials must be appointed, and even for 'small-entry' events it is advisable to have at least two referees, who can not only share the rather exacting demands of controlling these fast, non-stop games, but act as each other's time-keeper/scorer. Names and addresses of qualified referees can be obtained from the secretary of the County Football Association for the area in which the event is being staged. N.B. County F.A.s will only nominate referees for tournaments sanctioned by that Association or by the Football Association. (see Rules 'Sanctioning of Associations, Leagues, Competitions and Matches' in handbook published by the F.A.)

SPECTATORS

For the benefit of spectators attending Five-a-side Football events, programmes should be available which should contain the following information:-

Rules of play simply and concisely stated.
Full details of teams involved, viz. names, players' colours, etc.
Order of games and referees officiating.
Information about the competition and names of organisers.

SCOREBOARDS

It also adds to interest and enjoyment if spectators are kept informed of the state of games as they are played and, if the contest is being run on a league basis, team positions displayed periodically. For the most part, venues used for Five-a-side Football do not boast built-in scoreboards;

therefore such apparatus must be improvised. Public address systems can be used to announce such details, but not while play is actually in progress as this can be distracting to players and officials alike. Large time clocks, as used in ice hockey, would be a boon to Five-a-side Football tournaments!

TIMING

Timing is of vital importance as most major tournaments need to be organised to a tight schedule, so that a maximum number of games can be played in a limited period of time. Organisers, therefore, must ensure that games are played according to programme. Teams should be so marshalled that they are ready to enter the playing area as soon as a preceding game is ended, and egress from and entry to both the playing area and dressing rooms must be so arranged that 'change-over' can be effected with a minimum of delay.

TEAM COLOURS

Colours of teams participating should be determined well in advance of an event so that arrangements for dealing with clashes of colours can be decided. If teams were encouraged to be equipped with two sets of strips of different colours on entry to a competition, then few problems of this nature would be encountered.

FIRST AID

Though Five-a-side Football generally has proved to be remarkably free from incidents of serious injury to players, bruisings and abrasions to limbs and body are fairly common. This is due, of course, to the hard, non-resilient surfaces which surround playing areas, and though such injuries do not often incapacitate players they need immediate, on-the-spot treatment. Where the skin is broken especial care must be taken to clean and cover the wound so that the risk of infection is minimised.

Basic equipment, always readily to hand, should include:-

Sterilised, unmedicated dressings; small, medium and large.
Assorted wound dressings (at least 12).
Triangular bandages of unbleached calico, the longest side of which measures not less than 51 inches and each of the other sides not less than 36 inches.
Adhesive plaster 1 inch x 5 yards (2 rolls).
Half-ounce packets of absorbent, sterilised cotton wool(2).
Sterilised eye pad with bandage in sealed packet (2).
Assorted safety pins (12).
A pair of scissors with rounded ends to blades.

More serious injuries, such as fractures and deep lacerations, can occur and sometimes a hard-struck ball can cause injuries to faces and eyes of players and spectators alike. Because of such eventualities, organisers of tournaments are advised to enlist the services of one of the recognised First Aid organisations, i.e. St.John's (St.Andrew's in Scotland) or the British Red Cross.

ACKNOWLEDGEMENTS

For invaluable assistance, co-operation and encouragement, without which this book could not have been written, most grateful thanks are accorded to:-

Colleagues attached to divisional and local Associations of Youth Clubs throughout Great Britain.

Colleagues on the staff of the National Association of Youth Clubs.

The Football Association.

Sir Stanley Rous, C.B.E. JP

Those responsible for organising five-a-side football events on behalf of:

The National Association of Boys' Clubs.
The Methodist Youth Department.
The Boys' Brigade.

The Honorary Organising Secretary of:

The Daily Express, Great Britain Under 18 Five-a-side Football Championships.

The Manager of the Meadowbank Sports Centre, Edinburgh.

The Manager and Assistant Manager of the Harlow and District Sports Trust.

The Central Council of Physical Recreation.

Mr. G. Erik of Subbuteo Sports Games Ltd.

Mr. I.C. Cleave of Mitre Sports Limited.

Mr. H.C. Keele of J.F. Engineering Ltd.

Those players, officials, referees and spectators, too numerous to mention, involved in five-a-side football competitions up and down the country, whose advice and comments I consider to be of the utmost importance and to whom this publication is dedicated.

R.W. ELLIOT

THE LAST WORD!

'-Five-a-side football is now an established part of the British sporting scene and for thousands of players throughout the country, it constitutes a regular part of training in skill and fitness......

......In my travels throughout the world......it has become apparent to me that the five-a-side game is rapidly increasing in popularity and it is pleasing to see that Britain is well to the fore in this development-'

Stanley Rous.

SIR STANLEY ROUS, CBE JP
President of the Fédération
Internationale de Football
Association from 1961 to 1974.

Printed in England by Elsworth Bros. Ltd., Bowman Lane, Leeds LS10 1JD.